to Tocqueville the doors of the French Institute, and eventually of the Academy.

In 1837, when Alexis de Tocqueville had not been long settled in the old family chateau of his house, he came forward as a candidate for the representation of the *arrondisse-ment* of Valognes in his own depart-ment. His reception was not very flattering. A trace of the old revol[u]tionary prejudices lingered in the neighbourhood; a cry of *pas de nobles* was got up: his opponen[t] retired cotton-spinner who had a big house, said: "Prenez ga[rde] il va vous ramener les pige[ons]," pointing to the mighty dove[cot of] Tocqueville Manor; and, i[n fine,] the aristocratic though li[beral] candidate was defeated[.]

Two years later, at the [general] election of 1839, wher[e Tocque]ville had made his w[ay in his de]partment, and had [won the regard] of real attachment[...] neighbours and of[...] the country roun[d...] to the Chamber [by a] great majority, [...] his seat under [...] as long as ther[e was a par]liament in Fra[nce...] his was that t[...] be undermin[...] passions of t[he...] croached upon b[y...] of the Court, until [...] would remain, and [...] of the Parliamentary system would be followed at no distant time by

the despotism of a single ruler. At [leng]th the storm came. By no oth[er...] [ha]d it been so clearly f[...] [s]everal months [...]

difficulty of governing human affairs that a Constitution, now universally acknowledged to be a masterpiece of absurdity, was the work of several men of undoubted intellectual power and political [ins]ight. An attempt was made [by Tocque]ville to induce his col-[leagues to ado]pt the principle of a [...] but this and every [... to] construct the [... th]e Republican [...] failed. The [... turn]ed to a short-[... be]tween the frenzy [... so]cialism on the one [... v]iolence of that [reactio]n which speedily [... n]ame of Louis [B]onaparte.

[In the sum]mer of 1858 a more [serious a]ccident showed his lungs [af]fected. In the autumn he [was or]dered to a milder climate [than t]hat of his own well-beloved [Normand]in. He repaired to Cannes, [accom]panied by the devoted part-[ner] of his life, and by one or two [of] his nearest relatives and friends.

[O]n the 16th April, 1859, he expired. [B]y his own express desire his [m]ortal remains were interred in the churchyard of Tocqueville, and were attended to the grave by an immense assemblage, not of those who admired him for his genius, but of those who loved him for his goodness; and a plain cross of wood, after the fashion of the country, marks the spot where whatever of him was mortal lies.

DE LA
DÉMOCRATIE
EN AMÉRIQUE.

De ALBA, Joaquin. Joaquin de Alba Views Violence in America; De Tocqueville's America Revisited. Acropolis Books, 2400 17th St. N.W., Washington, D.C. 20009, 1969. 108p il (Americana by Acropolis) 70-75126. 6.95, 3.95 pa.

De Alba is a political cartoonist who worked until 1951 in his native Spain for the Franco regime. After 10 years in Latin America, he came to the U.S. in 1961 and for six years portrayed the passing political scene in the *Washington Daily News*. One hundred and thirty years before de Alba came to America, the distinguished French observer, Alexis de Tocqueville, visited our shores and wrote *Democracy in America*, a treatise which expressed the very essence of American character and institutions. Now de Alba has combined his visual art with the literary artistry of Tocqueville. *Violence in America* is a series of cartoons on current problems drawn by de Alba and appropriately captioned by passages from Tocqueville. This brilliant marriage of two art forms conceived more than a century apart demonstrates how little things have changed. Problems of racism and violence were predicted by Tocqueville and his commentary is as relevant as today's editorials. *Violence in America* is enjoyable and thought-provoking and is recommended for persons of all ages interested in the problems of our day.

CHOICE   JUNE'70
History, Geography &
Travel
North America

E
83 9.5
D27

Joaquin de Alba views

VIOLENCE in AMERICA

De Tocqueville's AMERICA REVISITED

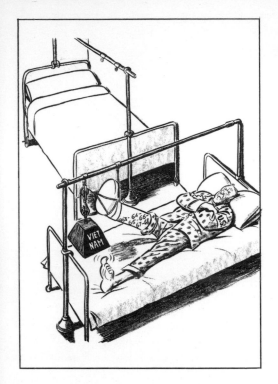

Joaquin de Alba views

VIOLENCE in AMERICA

[De Tocqueville's AMERICA REVISITED ★ ★]

Foreword by Chester Burger

© Joaquin de Alba 1969

PUBLISHED BY **Acropolis Books** / WASHINGTON, D.C.

contents

ACROPOLIS BOOKS
*Colortone Building, 2400 17th St., N.W.
Washington, D.C. 20009*

Printed in the United States of America by
Colortone Creative Printing, Washington, D.C. 20009

Type set in Century Schoolbook and Caledonia Bold.

Library of Congress Catalog Number 70-75126

Standard Book No.
    Paper 87491-120-6
    Hard Cover 87491-119-2

foreword

More than a few Europeans visited America a century ago, and a surprising number of them recorded their observations in diaries and in books. But none speaks to us today as does Alexis de Tocqueville. Under the rustic and often naive life of Nineteenth Century America, Alexis de Tocqueville perceived much of the essence of the American character. Although today our society is highly technological (and therefore our lives more dependent upon each other), and urbanized (only since 1920 have a majority of Americans lived in cities), the enduring characteristics that Alexis de Tocqueville noted remain today a major factor in our national life.

It is not too difficult to speak perceptively to one's contemporaries. It is a rare art to be understood by succeeding generations. Beethoven did it. Goya did it. These are the rare men whose perception strips away the transient, and the superficial, and who grasp the universality of human experiences.

Alexis de Tocqueville achieved also, in some degree, the difficult task of characterizing, not an individual, but an entire nation. Through his sensitivity, he recognized the essence of the American character.

Unquestionably, Alexis de Tocqueville's French origins added the necessary dimension of perspective. As he traveled across America by boat and stagecoach, he must have constantly made comparisons to the nation of his birth. For most of Alexis de Tocqueville's adult life, France was a Bourbon monarchy. Democracy —the idea that ordinary men could govern themselves better than any inherited ruler— challenged him, fascinated him, won him.

Joaquin de Alba has many of Alexis de Tocqueville's qualities, although we will need the passing of the years to confirm this.

De Alba, too, came from a land where democracy does not exist; indeed, he was a part of the machinery of Franco's Facist state. When he left Spain, he suffered not from poverty and hunger, but from the pains of a human spirit choking from lack of freedom of conscience and expression. (How barren the soil in which the seeds of liberty can take root!)

In America, Joaquin de Alba has looked at democracy with the same fascination and affection as his French predecessor. He has expressed himself with the brush rather than with the pen. In the pages of the *Washington Daily News,* he portrayed the passing scene.

But perhaps Joaquin de Alba has done something more. Perhaps he has gone beneath our proud pretensions, our talk of world leadership, our talk of democracy itself, to see the reality of American life today.

Langston Hughes, in his poem, "Let America be America Again," wrote:

> O, yes,
> I say it plain,
> America never was America to me.
> And yet I swear this oath—
> America will be!

This is the dream, and the hope, and the conviction of Joaquin de Alba. Only someone who is a friend could see us as we are and hold this faith. De Alba sees us too as we could be, and, I am certain, as we shall be.

Chester Burger

First, a story

A MAN WAS WALKING ALONG CARRYING A ROCK.

Once upon
a time...

then...

THE MEN WENT ON FIGHTING OVER THE ROCK
FOR THOUSANDS OF YEARS UNTIL SOLOMON,
THE WISE MAN, APPEARED AND SAID TO THEM:

"DON'T FIGHT ANYMORE. DIVIDE THE ROCK IN HALF."

and...

but...

CIVILIZATION HAD COME TO MANKIND, AND
SINCE THAT TIME LARGE NUMBERS OF MEN
HAVE BEEN SETTLING THEIR DIFFERENCES
BY DIVIDING THINGS IN HALVES . . .

Prologue

HOW I DISCOVERED AMERICA

By Joaquin de Alba
Translated from
Spanish by John Hoover

ON THAT NIGHT A HUGE ICEBERG was floating over the surface of the sea like a gigantic polar bear in search of his prey. The Titanic, unaware of its rendezvous with death, was aglow with light and gaiety as she glided toward the icy monster. Everybody knows what happened. The sea dragged the huge hulk down to the bottom and a fantastic vortex formed by the swirling water pulled hundreds of human beings under forever.

At least one human being arrived in the world during those hours of horror and death—
I was that one.

It would be pretentious to suggest that I was born to compensate for those who were lost. But I have always believed that I was born as one replacement.

In any event, my birth took place on that night of April 15, 1912, and the place chosen by my parents was the ancient Spanish city of Cadiz. I say chosen, because normally I would have been born in Seville, as had been planned, as my parents had been, as their three children who preceded me were, also the eight who came after me.

That was my first displacement.

Three months later my parents returned to Seville and lived there the rest of their lives. But I was not and am not a Sevillian.

Two years after I was born my mother had twins, and a sister of my father, Aunt Vicenta, took me to live with her to ease the burden weighing upon my poor mother. Thus began my second displacement, and this was twofold. It was, first, a displacement from the hearth of my parents, and second, a displacement from Seville, for my uncle was an official in Palma del Rio, a town in the province of Cordoba. Thereafter, I was separated from my parents, that is to say, I remained with my uncle and aunt. I spent most of my childhood and adolescence in that wonderful place which I still call my home town, although it really wasn't.

It is the home town of my wife, for the beautiful little girl who joined my childhood games was destined to become the sweet companion of all my years. It is also the home town of "El Cordobes," the most famous bullfighter of all time, who was born a few months after I was married in that city.

The American reader will not understand my emphasis on place of birth in a country approximately the size of Montana. *But let us consider it:* Within the enormous geographical expanse of the United States there is almost uniformity of custom and belief. It seems to me, the homogeneity of the American people and the stability of the union stem from the very differences of background within the country. Of course, there are many black people in the South; New York State has a concentration of Jews and people of Latin background; there are many Asians in California, and many Scandinavians in the northern Middle West. But it is also true that Negroes, Latins, Semites, Orientals, Slavs and Scandanavians are found throughout the United States in very even proportion, and at the same time the larger proportion of Anglo-Saxon whites to other groups is almost always maintained. Thus, no single group can overwhelmingly impose its personality or historic custom upon the rest. All, and each, influence the others and are, at the same time, influenced. This is America as I see it—one society with a single culture, personality, body of custom, and purpose.

The survival of the English language as the only tongue completes the unity. Even when, in the bosom of the family, the language of origin is spoken and thought, the youngsters soon manage to forget it and force their parents to speak English.

Furthermore, the rapid industrialization of the country with the mass production of consumer goods, of household goods, clothes, transportation, housing and the development of nationwide enterprises sets a general standard for all the country.

This is all united by an incomparable system of communication, which completes the picture of uniformity in an immense country, where to be born or brought up in one place or the other does not irrevocably stamp one with any fundamental or ineradicable difference.

Finally, we must not forget how young this country is. It could scarcely be called populated before the 18th Century.

Perhaps the American reader now can see the difference between this new land and ancient Spain—Spain which has a territory of 194,945 square miles compared to 3,615,211 square miles in America, and has a population of 150 per square mile compared to 55 in the United States.

Except for Switzerland, Spain is the most mountainous country of Europe. Because of this, some of the ancient civilizations which invaded the Iberian Peninsula halted and settled, rather than face crossing the range that blocked their horizon. In this way a great variety of character and custom developed among Spaniards and even among cities of Spain—Iberians, Phoenicians (these, 14 centuries before Christ), Greeks, Celts, Carthaginians, Romans, Visigoths, Moslems—all were tossed into the crucible to form the Spanish people.

Each of these civilizations left its definite mark in such a way that when finally the Moslems were defeated and expelled by the Catholic Monarchs, and Spanish unity was proclaimed, that unity had no greater scope than the purely legal and administrative. This is exactly the opposite of what occurred in the United States. In the United States, the only differences are legal and administrative, while in Spain the legal and administrative provide the only unity.

There is religion, of course. But such a rivalry exists between virgins, patrons, saints, and Christs that they seem more the standard bearers of warring legions than the symbols of a single religion. The Inquisition worked with such ardor for the religious unity of Spaniards that the Spanish became more Popish than the Pope. And with the multiplication of their representative effigies, religious unity was changed into a catalogue of religious separatism.

Spanish unification was decreed in 1469, a time when there were few roads and bridges, and communication between inhabitants of the peninsula was almost impossible, particularly since, as we have said, the country is so mountainous. Thus the various communities being isolated, each developed its own personality and created, each one, its own distinctive atmosphere.

The years passed. When the industrial revolution arrived in Europe, Spain was depopulated and had been bled by its adventurous conquest of the New World. It was, furthermore, more dedicated to the conversion of heretics, than the conversion of its economy through the building of factories.

But if this meant backwardness in the development of industrial and economic progress, the reverse is true of craftsmanship, which made great strides toward perfection, beauty, and individuality. Painting, dance, music, song, household goods, clothes, buildings, streets, plazas, cuisine, mosaic, embroidery, custom, character, and even the bread—all have a particular and different tradition in each corner of Spain.

This is why the point of origin of a Spaniard sets the style for the way of his life. Perhaps now the American reader will have a better understanding of my preoccupation with the place of my birth and with what I have called my displacement.

My parents lived in Seville on Reinoso Street in the Santa Cruz neighborhood, and, from time to time, they brought me from my home in Palma del Rio to spend a few days with them.

Santa Cruz is the most beautiful aggregation of streets and parks in the world. It is the old neighborhood, called the Jewish Quarter, where Seville's Jews lived during the Arab occupation. Their old traditions were the source of the greatest excitement I remember in my childhood. As I walked through the streets, I was aquiver with fantasy and mystery. I expected to see a witch pop out of every doorway and was sure a ghost lurked around each corner.

The narrowness of the Santa Cruz streets made the passage of vehicles difficult. For that reason it was a paradise for children whose mothers were always sure something was going to happen to them. We ran from the Plaza of Doña Elvira to the Gardens of Murillo, to the Santa Cruz Plaza and to the Patio of Flags, the main entrance of the castle of the Arab kings. Along the walls of the castle were huge beds of roses and colorful bell-flowers which climbed up over the windows and balconies of the houses facing them, forming a roof through which the sun's rays filtered. Old painters translated all that beauty to their canvases as I stood by them.

Already in those days, when I was six to eight years old, my greatest pleasure was to fill every scrap of paper I could get my hands on with grotesque figures. Those old street painters decided my vocation once and for all.

Some years later my elders sent me to the School of Fine Arts of Seville, and there I studied drawing and painting which, after more years, made me one of those painters.

But painting was not my true life's path. It was not the Virgins of Murillo nor the marvelous portraits of Velazquez which left their mark on my spirit. It was Goya. It was his bloody drawings which told of the Spanish tragedy under Napoleon's invasion. It was his "Caprices," his "Art of the Bullfight," and all the satire with which he interpreted the sadness, the joy, the picaresque, the candor of Spanish life during his time. It was his quick vision, his understanding of things made evident by the stroke of a pen, without the aid of color, which completely captivated me.

And that was the path, step by step, which brought me to the field of the political cartoon.

*   *   *

I GREATLY ADMIRE YOUNG REBELS— those who refuse to conform to the established patterns; those who can see that much of the traditional is old and worn out, even when it is not degrading. I admire them because they have looked at themselves in the mirror of history and have been able to see the value of youth. In their rebellion we may lose some of tomorrow's builders, but only through them can we find salvation. The young conformists are instruments of the past. The young rebels are guardians of the future.

Whenever a generation of young people moves into old age without having introduced some basic change into the historic process, God must weep.

Unfortunately, I was not a young rebel. I was a dreamer of the past. Dazzled by the beauty of the art of the past and overcome by the glories of the discovery and conquest of the New World, I thought more about past grandeur than about future progress. In addition to this, my family tradition was conservative. Consequently, I began to work in the Seville press as a conservative political cartoonist.

By this time Spain was a monarchy without subjects. Alfonso XIII was a king without authority, and, facing a multitude before his palace demanding that he abdicate—he renounced the throne and went into exile. His fall, unfortunately, brought in a regime just as inept—a republic without citizens.

Spain was split in two. On one side, the starving, and on the other, the overfed. In between, a group of inefficient officials tried, but were unable to operate effectively.

It was the moment for my third displacement, and without thinking much about it, I moved to Madrid, taking with me my portfolio of political cartoons and the illusions of my 19 years.

It will not surprise anyone that, being a young conservative, I put my talent at the disposal of my affluent friends. However—and I haven't changed—if I wasn't one of the hungry, I wasn't one of the overfed. But as I've already said, I was not a young rebel and, furthermore, I knew that the poor man in Spain eats the crumbs from the feasts of the rich at the cost of standing to heel as a loyal dog.

When Spain abandoned feudalism, the great lords hired those who had been their vassals much the same way as later, in this country, the plantation owners hired the freed Negro slaves. "Now you are free," they said. "Each one may do whatever he can." And the Spanish people were abandoned to their fate, left at the mercy of their old masters who, of course, continued to own the land.

The freed Negro, indeed, had a great advantage. The United States was rapidly industrializing. Great public works were under way, and throughout the Union new fountains of wealth and progress flowed freely. The American Negro could choose among many opportunities to sell his labor. But the Spanish came out of feudalism in an era when industry was small and rudimentary, and could provide work for only a few. Thus the great mass of free Spanish men had to sell their labor for work in the fields, or in other services to the lords, or as soldiers in the ever-continuing wars of expansion of Spanish monarchs. They, of course, could not set the price for their labor, but had to accept whatever was offered, as the number competing for work was great.

This subservience continued with little change until the Spanish Republic was proclaimed in 1931. The economically depressed classes then organized into political parties and labor unions; they then began to exercise strong pressure on the owners of wealth, trying to change the social structure of Spain in their favor. *A useless effort!* The economic power of the ruling classes, and the tightly controlled interests, built up over the centuries, formed an almost impregnable

bulwark. The wealthy redoubled their propaganda efforts using all means, particularly the press, where I worked in triumph—having made my name well-known during the six years of the Republic.

On July 18, 1936, General Franco took up arms against the Republic, and I put my efforts at his service. When the Spanish Civil War was over, my name was honored in Franco Spain, and because of this I was entrusted with the editorial cartoon of *Arriba* of Madrid, the official organ of Spain's only party—that which General Franco headed.

I worked loyally for several years, but disillusionment and spiritual breakdown pressed heavily upon me. The political intrigues within the National Movement and my utter conviction that a one-party system was not the climate in which I could continue my work brought me to the decision to leave Spain—that Spain which once again had proclaimed a union of men and country as in the Sixteenth Century, but which divided the people into the conquerors and the conquered, into the "Nationals" and the "Reds", into those who had the right to speak and those who had to keep silent, into those who took all the credit and those who had all the blame, and finally into those who could curse and those who could only sigh.

When I went away, my wife and son, indeed, all that I loved, remained behind for a time, but a star firmly guided the pilot of my ship— freedom of conscience and expression.

As I went along, one conviction came through indelibly—the idea that a single party system in some cases can settle economic and technical problems, but never problems of the spirit.

It was a clear May morning in 1951 when my own "Santa Maria" cast anchor on the left bank of the Hudson.

TRAVELING TO AMERICA ON AN IMMIGRANT ship is a fascinating experience. I came to the United States as a visitor, but most of the passengers on the Italian vessel, the "Saturnia," were emigrants from various parts of Europe. It was a broad human spectrum, many tongues, many physical characteristics, many attitudes.

The ship sailed from Genoa, but I boarded at Barcelona. Throughout most of a day's sailing the interest of the passengers was consumed in watching the coast of Spain, which we circumnavigated, to finally land in Lisbon before beginning the eight-day voyage across the Atlantic.

During the first day the passengers huddled for security in their own national groups. They produced musical instruments and with song and dance spread joy throughout the ship. But as the days passed, the groups began to mix. They learned to communicate in some mysterious way in an idiom that sprang mostly from willingness. A number of Italians could be seen doing Slavic dances while Greeks sang "O Sole Mio." In this common spirit of hope, the time passed until the day before we were due to arrive in New York. On that day nobody left his quarters. It was as if the sea had swallowed everyone. Only the children, generally unmindful of life's consequences, continued to run about the decks, laughing and playing in the ways of childhood, a practice that is also a sort of common language.

The passengers seemed almost like lovers who finally face the fact that this is the last day of their love affair. All the laughter, the singing, and the dancing was over, and with it, the brotherhood born of common grief and common joy.

There was little sleep aboard ship that night. Before dawn every passenger was scanning the horizon. A pale red light broke over the rectangular piers of Manhattan, and a noisy stream of cars along Henry Hudson Parkway seemed to bid us welcome.

Now, on the point of disembarking, the emigrants again pounded each other on the shoulders and wept. Some, because they could discern loved ones who were waiting for them on the dock below; others, because no one was waiting for them; and all, because in that moment the great distance between them and the ones they left behind was irrevocably established. To emigrate is to split the soul, I thought. The price of freedom is very high for those who are poor.

THE SHORTEST DISTANCE between two points is that which leaves $10 in the pocket of the taxi driver, and that is what the one who took me to my hotel departed with. It was some time before I realized I had paid $7 too much. It may seem a small item to include in one's life story, but not when it is realized that $80 was all I had for my conquest of America, and now I had only $70.

Along with my poverty, I had a total ignorance of English, a combination which surely must have put me in a class for recklessness with skyjumpers. However, for a Spaniard, tribulation is the way of life. As he encounters one difficulty he cannot subdue, like the hurdler, he passes over it to take another in stride. Thus, the Spanish have developed as their most outstanding trait a sense of improvisation—that and individuality. Mexico was not conquered, nor the Andes by troops moving according to strategic plan.

There were no troops, nor was there strategy. A handful of Spaniards advanced toward the unknown, experienced chiefly in bypassing difficulty. Always, the improvisation of one was the salvation of the rest. History tells us that, in the case of Mexico, Hernan Cortés burned his ships to make retreat impossible. I didn't have to burn them, for, in a sense, I had swum the Atlantic.

Fortunately, friendship is one of the Spanish virtues. I found three friends in New York, the Royo brothers, Rodrigo and Vicente, who were the U. S. correspondents of Spanish publications, and Rafael Pallares, a hairdresser who had come over some 30 years before. Because of their knowledge of the country, their encouragement, their advice, and their generosity, my opportunities were not exhausted as quickly as the initial $70.

There was a period of unsuccessful attempts at employment in New York and Washington. It only served to give me a general impression at first hand of what the United States is. There are those who say first impressions are the most nearly accurate. Whether or not this is so, my first notion of the United States was this: *the United States is a train one has to catch.* A very powerful engine, its natural wealth, pulls a string of passenger cars with freight cars in the rear. The whole train responds to a strong forward movement—a very dynamic one. It goes at headlong speed. One who wants to get on a particular coach has to be extremely able. He must run alongside the train at an equal speed, and he must have great luck. But it is very difficult. More than one have perished in the attempt. There's an easier way: grab whatever car you can, which is likely to be at the rear—the car where the dishes are washed. Later you can move forward if you get the chance.

This is the way I viewed America then, and I still do.

On the other hand, it sometimes happens, though rarely, that a number of favorable circumstances coincide, and the wayfairing stranger manages to board the train at exactly the right coach. He is inside. The effort has been great, and fate has been kind. Everything around him seems to sing of victory. Then, a few miles further along—how, one doesn't know —some centrifugal force throws him off. This happened to me, and with this book I am trying once more to climb aboard, on a different car.

To explain I will have to make a slight detour.

Convinced that it would not be profitable to remain in the United States, and goaded by economic problems (the conventions of the American system, which includes distrust of foreigners, simply dismissed my qualifications, and I was further hampered in my search for even routine work by the restrictions of my visitor's visa), I decided, again with the help of my friends, to go to Latin America. I had great hopes of prospering there because the language was my own, and because it was a developing area where my skills would be welcome. So, with portfolio of paintings under my arm, I set out for the land that once was part of a vast Spanish empire.

My experience in Latin America greatly enriched my understanding of the world, and there is much to write about it. But that's another book. It has no place here. It is enough to say that there I was reunited with my wife and son; that I was fortunate and successful; and that on April 19, 1961, I returned to the United States, this time accompanied by my wife, but again without my son, who had gone back to Spain to pursue his study of philosophy.

This time I was better prepared, having brought a collection of political cartoons, in English, which I considered to be in American taste.

Somebody had given me a letter to the editor of the *Washington Daily News,* a Scripps-Howard newspaper, and this I presented to Nicholas Blatchford, then Assistant Managing Editor, who received us (my wife had gone with me). I showed him my drawings, and with his kind and intelligent smile, he took them to the editor, at that time, John T. O'Rourke. When he came back, he purchased two of the cartoons and told me to come back the next Monday (it was Friday), for the editor wanted to talk to me. Nobody can imagine the joy with which we left the office where thereafter I was to work for six years. I had earned my first money in the United States the day after we had arrived.

It was exhilarating—to seek to climb aboard the American train at exactly the coach of my choice, and to find Mr. Blatchford in the doorway holding out a hand. It was something that happens only once in a lifetime. To him, with his fine talent; to the great enthusiasm of Mr. O'Rourke; to the friendship and understanding of John Hoover, who helped me with my language problems—to these I owe the experience of working for the free American press, having signed more than 1,000 editorial cartoons in the capital of the United States.

Six years later, as I have said, the retirement of Mr. O'Rourke and the succession of another editor (whose name I do not care to remember), created the centrifugal force which threw me off the train.

*　　*　　*

EVERY COUNTRY HAS ITS DARK SIDE for the foreigner, and that of the United States is its expansionist policy. What can be said about the truth of the worldwide opinion was never a matter of great preoccupation for me. On the one hand, I know that those countries which are not expansionist are not so, largely because internal weakness makes it a problem for them to defend their own boundaries. On the other hand, because expansion is not necessarily evil in itself, it depends upon the way it is carried out whether it brings blessings or curses. Napoleon broadened the horizons of freedom, and Hitler those of tyranny; Rome extended culture, and the barbarians destroyed it; Spain extended religion, and England, commerce. One assumes that the United States is the *bearer* of *democracy, freedom,* and the *fountain of riches*. In short, these are three pillars of the country —and that was my hope and the faith I put in America's destiny. Consequently, when I worked for the *Washington Daily News,* I devoted myself completely to the defense of these high ideals, aided by the absolute freedom given me on the paper to carry out my work.

President John F. Kennedy was a Democratic president in every sense of the word. His name and his fortune helped him greatly in his climb to power, but he had enough ability, training, and personality to maintain it in his own right. And, above all, he was an honest man. He had not discarded the U. S. policy of expansionism in his programs, but he tried to accomplish it with principle. "No dictatorship of the left or of the right" was his formula in world affairs. He had faith in liberty and confronted communism with that as his armor. For this reason he originated programs of aid and development which were designed to raise the lowest standards of life.

In domestic affairs he realized the time had come to extend civil rights in completion of the work of Abraham Lincoln—for reasons of justice and for reasons of practical necessity. It was the same policy he pursued in foreign affairs applied to internal matters: strengthening democracy to protect it from communism without running the risk of war. He had pursued several other important policies, including completion of the treaty banning the atmospheric testing of nuclear devices, which put the brakes on the dreadful arms race clouding man's future, and development of an imaginative and skillful space program—an area in which the Soviets had made great progress.

On the afternoon of November 22, 1963, the clamorous keys of the teletype machines spelled out the horror of his assassination in Dallas. At that moment all my hopes and aspirations were shattered. If the man, who at his highest level in the nation had tried to bring a sense of dignity to the weak (the same dignity which he, himself, possessed), could be cut down in so disgraceful a way, what hope was there for men of good will? What hope for me?

The mournful shroud which covered President Kennedy's body darkened the rebirth of humanity which had just begun to glimmer. The forward movement of humanity is always beset by repressive forces, and often has to pause, or even retreat. President Kennedy's death did not kill all hope, but it sidetracked the humanitarian surge for a generation. As a result there are many who will suffer to the end of their days.

The American press has a marked tendency to wrap up in a single term many different things. The word "violence" is such a term. There is an attempt to reduce all manner of events to a common denominator in such a way that the particular value of each is overlooked. This is part of a predigested picture which the American people receive.

It was evident that certain programs, among them Civil Rights, the Nuclear Test Ban Treaty, the Alliance for Progress, restrictions put on the Bay of Pigs landing, and the refusal to recognize certain Latin American governments imposed by military coup—had created hatreds against the New Frontier. But when President Kennedy was assassinated, the stereotype offered in explanation was wrapped up in the simplistic term, "violence." Thus the national Calvary which most of us suffered was explained by attributing it, imprecisely, to a general atmosphere of "violence." The causes behind the violence remained unspoken, if not hidden.

In Vietnam, escalation of the war has brought in consequence as much violence at home as there.

On another day, April 4, 1968, Dr. Martin Luther King, Jr., Nobel Prize winner, was, himself, assassinated in Memphis, Tennessee. I have nothing further to say of that hideous crime, for the entire world has condemned it. It is enough to point out that it was the man who led American Negroes along the path of "non-violence" who was destroyed by violence. It was not only Negroes who had found a brave and capable leader in Martin Luther King. In him the nation had gained the one man it needed to lead the Negro people. His loss, which seemed so great for those of his race, was indeed much greater for the white people and for the country.

Finally, the death on June 6, 1968, of Senator Robert F. Kennedy rounded out a period of anarchy and disgrace unequalled in the modern history of the United States. It is possible that Senator Kennedy would never have been elected President of the United States, but his assassin made it certain. Democracy, the freedom of the American people to elect whom they wished, was thwarted by the assassin's bullet. Thereafter, the word "violence" took on an even more sinister connotation.

It was in that moment that I decided to undertake this book. For four months I worked in Washington on the theme under a cloud of grief and guided only by an ideal of justice and a faith in the values of freedom.

So much for my life story. However, I must give the reader a little broader explanation of my points of view.

At this moment, I suppose I am disillusioned by the unrelieved panorama of violence. One must also suppose that I believe that freedom and democracy in the world can be endangered by those who make a mockery of it in their own country. But if these are sufficient reasons for soul-searching, there are other reasons and other hopes which inspire and motivate me.

A people capable of bringing to fruition this gigantic, forward-moving spirit —the United States—cannot perish in the whirlwind of racial passion. The creative genius of America cannot die in an artificial fire. The people who had the determination and energy to overcome the slaveholders of the South, cannot be conquered by their own. The story is not yet told, and freedom has not become the legacy of those who have no soul. I can still produce this book in the name of freedom of conscience and expression.

Such is the great advantage of democracy over a single-party system. It is the difference between a "pacified" Spain and a conclusive America. Here, I can produce this book making a valid comparison between the two countries, while in Spain I could only pass judgment on the United States. Besides, one must not forget that the Spanish peace of the past 28 years was purchased at the cost of one million dead. The United States also had to sacrifice 600,000 lives in the Civil War, but that was to free the Negro slaves. It was a forward step that the country now seeks to extend. The Spanish Civil War was fought to stop the march of the Spanish people toward human dignity. It led to a stagnation that one despairs of ever dissolving.

*   *   *

WELL, LET US NOW RETURN to those emigrants who came over with us 17 years ago. What has happened to them?

I am sure that those who wept when they first saw the port of New York soon ceased to weep. The great American power of assimilation would soon make itself felt. In a short time the emigrants would become part of the common American scene because, with an income which brings security, there is also a determination to maintain status and extend the security to their children. They are free and proud citizens. They are able to think, and have the right to express their thoughts. They remember the old country with a sweet sadness. They remember past suffering as a nightmare, and are convinced of all the dogmatic truths of pragmatic America in living up to their new status as part of the American mass.

But what about their children, those who who played on the decks, pummeling each other, exchanging the common language of laughter? Now they will be in their twenties. What a wonderful age! Probably more than one is rebelling. Most of them will be heartbroken at the murder of "Bobby." Many probably have decorated their cars with daisies.

Will one of them, at least, have gone to sleep forever in Vietnam while dreaming of that ship?

Joaquin de Alba

Violence appears

●● The Negro, who is plunged in this abyss of evils, scarcely feels his own calamitous situation. Violence made him a slave, and the habit of servitude gives him the thoughts and desires of a slave; he admires his tyrants more than he hates them, and finds his joy and his pride in the servile imitation of those who oppress him: his understanding is degraded to the level of his soul. ●●

Vol. 1 / Chapter XVIII
DEMOCRACY IN AMERICA
—Alexis de Tocqueville (1805-1859)

●● Complaints are made in France that the number of suicides increases; in America suicide is rare, but insanity is said to be more common than anywhere else. These are all different symptoms of the same disease. ●●

Vol. 2 / Chapter XIII (SECOND BOOK)
DEMOCRACY IN AMERICA
—Alexis de Tocqueville (1805-1859)

●● A revolution which overthrows an ancient regal family, in order to place men of more recent growth at the head of a democratic people, may temporarily weaken the central power; but however anarchical such a revolution may appear at first, we need not hesitate to predict that its final and certain consequence will be to extend and to secure the prerogatives of that power. ●●

Vol. 2 / Chapter IV (FOURTH BOOK)
DEMOCRACY IN AMERICA
—Alexis de Tocqueville (1805-1859)

SATURN DEVOURS HIS SONS

●● It may readily be conceived, that if men, passionately bent upon physical gratifications, desire eagerly, they are also easily discouraged: as their ultimate object is to enjoy, the means to reach that object must be prompt and easy, or the trouble of acquiring the gratification would be greater than the gratification itself. ●●

Vol. 2 / Chapter XIII (SECOND BOOK)
DEMOCRACY IN AMERICA
—Alexis de Tocqueville (1805-1859)

LEFT   MIDDLE   RIGHT

POLITICAL ASSASSINATION

&& Amongst democratic nations men easily attain a certain equality of conditions: they can never attain the equality they desire. It perpetually retires from before them, yet without hiding itself from their sight, and in retiring draws them on. At every moment they think they are about to grasp it; it escapes at every moment from their hold. They are near enough to see its charms, but too far off to enjoy them; and before they have fully tasted its delights, they die.'' &&

Vol. 2 / Chapter XIII (SECOND BOOK)
DEMOCRACY IN AMERICA
—Alexis de Tocqueville (1805-1859)

●● They are more apt to
complete a number of under-
takings with rapidity, than to
raise lasting monuments of their
achievements; and they care
much more for success than for
fame. What they most ask of
men is obedience,—what they
most covet is empire. ●●

Vol. 2 / Chapter XIX (THIRD BOOK)
DEMOCRACY IN AMERICA
—Alexis de Tocqueville (1805-1859)

66 The remedy for the vices of the army is not to be found in the army itself, but in the country. Democratic nations are naturally afraid of disturbance and of despotism; the object is to turn these natural instincts into well-digested, deliberate, and lasting tastes. When men have at last learned to make a peaceful and profitable use of freedom, and have felt its blessings,—when they have conceived a manly love of order, and have freely submitted themselves to discipline,—these same men, if they follow the profession of arms, bring into it, unconsciously and almost against their will, these same habits and manners. 99

Vol. 2 / Chapter XXII (THIRD BOOK)
DEMOCRACY IN AMERICA
—Alexis de Tocqueville (1805-1859)

"DEMOCRACY IS COMING!!"

66 If peace is peculiarly hurtful to democratic armies, war secures to them advantages which no other armies ever possess; and these advantages, however little felt at first, cannot fail in the end to give them the victory. 99

Vol. 2 / Chapter XXIV (THIRD BOOK)
DEMOCRACY IN AMERICA
—Alexis de Tocqueville (1805-1859)

"DEMOCRACY IS HERE!!"

❝ We have seen, on the contrary, that amongst a democratic people the choicer minds of the nation are gradually drawn away from the military profession, to seek by other paths distinction, power, and especially wealth. ❞

Vol. 2 / Chapter XXIV (THIRD BOOK)
DEMOCRACY IN AMERICA
—Alexis de Tocqueville (1805-1859)

"HOW WONDERFUL FOR THOSE WHO SURVIVE!"

●● A people which has existed for centuries under a system of castes and classes can only arrive at a democratic state of society by passing through a long series of more or less critical transformations, accomplished by violent efforts, and after numerous vicissitudes; in the course of which, property, opinions, and power are rapidly transferred from one hand to another. ●●

Vol. 2 / Chapter XXI (THIRD BOOK)
DEMOCRACY IN AMERICA
—Alexis de Tocqueville (1805-1859)

"MY MOTHER SAYS MY BROTHER IS IN JAIL FOR BURNING BUILDINGS IN WASHINGTON!"

❝ As the spread of equality, taking place in several countries at once, simultaneously impels their various inhabitants to follow manufactures and commerce, not only do their tastes grow alike, but their interests are so mixed and entangled with one another, that no nation can inflict evils on other nations without those evils falling back upon itself; and all nations ultimately regard war as a calamity, almost as severe to the conqueror as to the conquered. ❞

Vol. 2 / Chapter XXVI (THIRD BOOK)
DEMOCRACY IN AMERICA
—Alexis de Tocqueville (1805-1859)

50

●● War is nevertheless an oc-currence to which all nations are subject, democratic nations as well as others. Whatever taste they may have for peace, they must hold themselves in readiness to repel aggression, or in other words they must have an army. ●●

Vol. 2 / Chapter XXII (THIRD BOOK)
DEMOCRACY IN AMERICA
—Alexis de Tocqueville (1805-1859)

The little society

THE BEGINNING

●● Democratic liberty is far from accomplishing all the projects it undertakes with the skill of an adroit despotism. It frequently abandons them before they have borne their fruits, or risks them when the consequences may prove dangerous; but in the end it produces greater results than any absolute government. It does fewer things well, but it does a greater number of things. ●●

Vol. 2 / Introduction
DEMOCRACY IN AMERICA
—Alexis de Tocqueville (1805-1859)

❝ It is not by the exercise of power or by the habit of obedience that men are debased; it is by the exercise of a power which they believe to be illegitimate, and by obedience to a rule which they consider to be usurped and unjust. ❞

Vol. 1 / Introduction
DEMOCRACY IN AMERICA
—Alexis de Tocqueville (1805-1859)

THE GRANDFATHERS

●● I have also had occasion to show how the increasing love of well-being, and the fluctuating character of property cause democratic nations to dread all violent disturbance. The love of public tranquillity is frequently the only passion which these nations retain, and it becomes more active and powerful amongst them in proportion as all other passions droop and die. This naturally disposes the members of the community constantly to give or to surrender additional rights to the central power, which alone seems to be interested in defending them by the same means that it uses to defend itself. ●●

Vol. 2 / Chapter III (FOURTH BOOK)
DEMOCRACY IN AMERICA
—Alexis de Tocqueville (1805-1859)

66 The man of a democratic age is extremely reluctant to obey his neighbour who is his equal; he refuses to acknowledge in such a person ability superior to his own; he mistrusts his justice, and is jealous of his power; he fears and he condemns him; and he loves continually to remind him of the common dependence in which both of them stand to the same master. 99

Vol. 2 / Chapter III (FOURTH BOOK)
DEMOCRACY IN AMERICA
—Alexis de Tocqueville (1805-1859)

OPEN HOUSING

❝ Amongst the laws which rule human societies there is one which seems to be more precise and clear than all others. If men are to remain civilized, or to become so, the

art of associating together must grow and improve, in the same ratio in which the equality of conditions is increased. ●●

Vol. 2 / Chapter V (SECOND BOOK)
DEMOCRACY IN AMERICA
—Alexis de Tocqueville (1805-1859)

HEADACHE

66 I am well aware that in this respect public institutions may themselves do much; they may encourage or repress the tendencies which originate in the state of society. I therefore do not maintain, I repeat, that a people is secure from revolutions simply because conditions are equal in the community; but I think that, whatever the institutions of such a people may be, great revolutions will always be far less violent and less frequent than is supposed; and I can easily discern a state of polity, which, when combined with the principle of equality, would render society more stationary than it has been in our western part of the world. 99

Vol. 2 / Chapter XXI (THIRD BOOK)
DEMOCRACY IN AMERICA
—Alexis de Tocqueville (1805-1859)

●● If ever America undergoes great revolutions, they will be brought about by the presence of the black race on the soil of the United States,—that is to say, they will owe their origin, not to the equality, but to the inequality, of conditions. ●●

Vol. 2 / Chapter XXI (THIRD BOOK)
DEMOCRACY IN AMERICA
—Alexis de Tocqueville (1805-1859)

THE DANGEROUS POOR

❝ Almost all the revolutions which have changed the aspect of nations have been made to consolidate or to destroy social inequality. Remove the secondary causes which have produced the great convulsions of the world, and you will almost always find the principle of inequality at the bottom. Either the poor have attempted to plunder the rich, or the rich to enslave the poor. If then a state of society can ever be founded in which every man shall have something to keep, and little to take from others, much will have been done for the peace of the world. ❞

Vol. 2 / Chapter XXI (THIRD BOOK)
DEMOCRACY IN AMERICA
—Alexis de Tocqueville (1805-1859)

A majority taken collectively may be regarded as a being whose opinions, and most frequently whose interests, are opposed to those of another being, which is styled a minority. If it be admitted that a man, possessing absolute power, may misuse that power by wronging his adversaries, why should a majority not be liable to the same reproach?

Vol. 1 / Chapter XV
DEMOCRACY IN AMERICA
—Alexis de Tocqueville (1805-1859)

BLACK POWER

❝ The most formidable of all the ills which threaten the future existence of the Union, arises from the presence of a black population upon its territory; and in contemplating the cause of the present embarassments or of the future dangers of the United States, the observer is invariably led to consider this as a primary fact. ❞

Vol. 1 / Chapter XVIII
DEMOCRACY IN AMERICA
—Alexis de Tocqueville (1805-1859)

66 When military service is compulsory, the burden is indiscriminately and equally borne by the whole community. This is another necessary consequence of the social condition of these nations, and of their notions. The government may do almost whatever it pleases, provided it appeals to the whole community at once: it is the unequal distribution of the weight, not the weight itself, which commonly occasions resistance. 99

Vol. 2 / Chapter XXIII (THIRD BOOK)
DEMOCRACY IN AMERICA
—Alexis de Tocqueville (1805-1859)

YESTERDAY

"YOU ARE AN AFRICAN!"

The principle of equality, which makes men independent of each other, gives them a habit and a taste for following, in their private actions, no other guide but their own will. This complete independence, which they constantly enjoy towards their equals and in the inter-course of private life, tends to make them look upon all authority with a jealous eye, and speedily suggests to them the notion and the love of political freedom.

Vol. 2 / Chapter I (FOURTH BOOK)
DEMOCRACY IN AMERICA
—Alexis de Tocqueville (1805-1859)

TODAY

"ARE YOU AN AFRICAN?"

Blow-up

●● I think that in our time it is very necessary to cleanse, to regulate, and to adapt the feeling of ambition, but that it would be extremely dangerous to seek to impoverish and to repress it over-much. We should attempt to lay down certain extreme

limits, which it should never be allowed to outstep; but its range within those established limits should not be too much checked. 99

Vol. 2 / Chapter XIX (THIRD BOOK)
DEMOCRACY IN AMERICA
—Alexis de Tocqueville (1805-1859)

❝ We do not, therefore, see in the United States a numerous and always turbulent crowd, who, regarding the law as their natural enemy, view it with no eyes but those of fear and suspicion. It is impossible, on the contrary, not to see that the mass of the people evince a great confidence in the legislation which governs the country, and feel for it a sort of paternal affection. ❞

Vol. 2 / Chapter XIX (Third Book)
DEMOCRACY IN AMÈRICA
—Alexis de Tocqueville (1805-1859)

66 Although the Americans are constantly modifying or abrogating some of their laws, they by no means display revolutionary passions. It may be easily seen, from the promptitude with which they check and calm themselves when public excitement begins to grow alarming, and at the very moment when passions seem most roused, that they dread a revolution as the worst of misfortunes, and that every one of them is inwardly resolved to make great sacrifices to avoid such a catastrophe. In no country in the world is the love of property more active and more anxious than in the United States; nowhere does the majority display less inclination for those principles which threaten to alter, in whatever manner, the laws of property. **99**

Vol. 2 / Chapter XXI (THIRD BOOK)
DEMOCRACY IN AMERICA
—Alexis de Tocqueville (1805-1859)

THE FLAG OF ROBERT F. KENNEDY

THE HOPE OF MILLIONS OF PEOPLES

●● When I refuse to obey an unjust law, I do not contest the right which the majority has of commanding, but I simply appeal from the sovereignty of the people to the sovereignty of mankind. It has been asserted that a people can never entirely outstep the boundaries of justice and of reason in those affairs which are more peculiarly its own; and that consequently full power may fearlessly be given to the majority by which it is represented. But this language is that of a slave. ●●

Vol. 1 / Chapter XV
DEMOCRACY IN AMERICA
—Alexis de Tocqueville (1805-1859)

&& I will readily admit that the mass of the people very sincerely desire the good of the country. . . . &&

Vol. 2 / Introduction
DEMOCRACY IN AMERICA
—Alexis de Tocqueville (1805-1859)

LAW AND ORDER

❝ Among the immense multitude who, in the United States, crowd into the career of politics, I have seen very few who evinced that manly candour, that vigorous independence of thought, which has often distinguished the Americans of former times, and which, wherever it is found, is as it were the salient feature of a great character. ❞

Vol. 1 / Introduction
DEMOCRACY IN AMERICA
—Alexis de Tocqueville (1805-1859)

Top secret report

66 When an opinion is represented by a society, it necessarily assumes a more exact and explicit form. It numbers its partisans, and compromises their welfare in its cause: they, on the other hand, become acquainted with each other, and their zeal is increased by their number. 99

Vol. 1 / Chapter XII
DEMOCRACY IN AMERICA
—Alexis de Tocqueville (1805-1859)

66 Even after this great revolution is consummated, the revolutionary habits engendered by it may long be traced, and it will be followed by deep commotion. As all this takes place at the very time at which social conditions are becoming more equal, it is inferred that some concealed relation and secret tie exists between the principle of equality itself and revolution, insomuch that the one cannot exist without giving rise to the other. 99

Vol. 2 / Chapter XXI (THIRD BOOK)
DEMOCRACY IN AMERICA
—Alexis de Tocqueville (1805-1859)

66 In aristocracies men have often much greatness and strength of their own; when they find themselves at variance with the greater number of their fellow-countrymen, they withdraw to their own circle, where they support and console themselves. Such is not the case in a democratic country; there, public favour seems as necessary as the air we breathe, and to live at variance with the multitude is, as it were, not to live. 99

Vol. 2 / Chapter XXI (THIRD BOOK)
DEMOCRACY IN AMERICA
—Alexis de Tocqueville (1805-1859)

Law enforcement

INVESTED INTEREST

●● It is believed by some that modern society will be ever changing its aspect; for myself, I fear that it will ultimately be too invariably fixed in the same institutions, the same prejudices, the same manners, so that mankind will be stopped and circumscribed; that the mind will swing backwards and forwards for ever, without begetting fresh ideas; that man will waste his strength in bootless and solitary trifling; and, though in continual motion, that humanity will cease to advance. ●●

Vol. 2 / Chapter XXI (THIRD BOOK)
DEMOCRACY IN AMERICA
—Alexis de Tocqueville (1805-1859)

GUN LAW

66 This is surprising at first sight, but a more attentive investigation explains the fact. I do not think that it is as easy as is supposed to uproot the prejudices of a democratic people—to change its belief— to supersede principles once established, by new principles in religion, politics, and morals —in a word, to make great and frequent changes in men's minds. 99

Vol. 2 / Chapter XXI (THIRD BOOK)
DEMOCRACY IN AMERICA
—Alexis de Tocqueville (1805-1859)

Military hospital

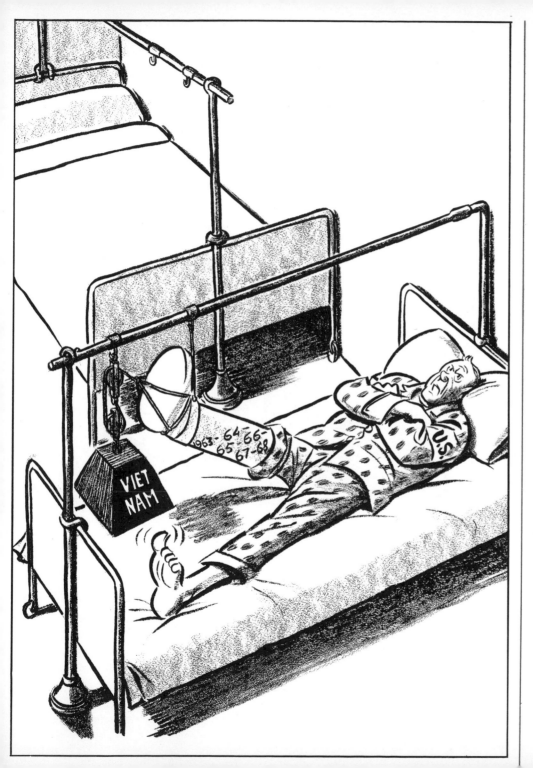

66 In a previous part of the same letter, Washington makes the following admirable and just remark: 'The nation which indulges towards another an habitual hatred, or an habitual fondness, is in some degree a slave. It is a slave to its animosity or to its affection, either of which is sufficient to lead it astray from its duty and its interest. 99

Vol. 2 / Chapter XXVI (Fourth Book)
DEMOCRACY IN AMERICA
—Alexis de Tocqueville (1805-1859)

66 Thus, on the one hand, it is extremely difficult in democratic ages to draw nations into hostilities; but, on the other hand, it is almost impossible that any two of them should go to war without embroiling the rest. The interests of all are so interlaced, their opinions and their wants so much alike, that none can remain quiet when the others stir. Wars, therefore, become more rare, but when they break out they spread over a larger field.

Vol. 2 / Chapter XXVI (Fourth Book)
DEMOCRACY IN AMERICA
—Alexis de Tocqueville (1805-1859)

Presidential campaign 1968

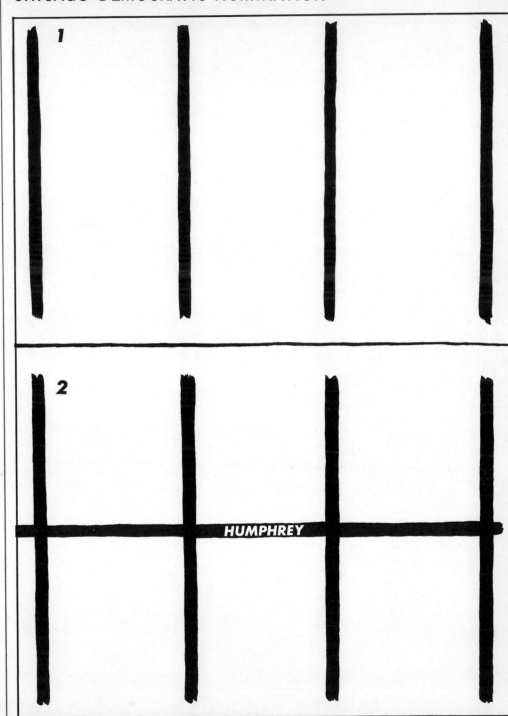

66 I may here be met by an objection, derived from electioneering intrigues, the meannesses of candidates, and the calumnies of their opponents. These are opportunities of animosity which occur the oftener the more frequent elections become. Such evils are, doubtless, great, but they are transient; whereas the benefits which attend them remain. The desire of being elected may lead

3

4

some men for a time to mutual
hostility; but this same desire
leads all men, in the long run,
mutually to support each other;
and if it happens that an election accidentally severs two
friends, the electoral system
brings a multitude of citizens
permanently together who
would always have remained
unknown to each other. Freedom
engenders private animosities,
but despotism gives birth to
general indifference. . . . 99

Vol. 2 / Introduction
DEMOCRACY IN AMERICA
—Alexis de Tocqueville (1805-1859)

THE VICTORS

●● Democracy does not confer the most skilful kind of government upon the people, but it produces that which the most skilful governments are frequently unable to awaken, namely, an all-pervading and restless activity—a super-abundant force—an energy which is never seen elsewhere, and which may, under favourable circumstances, beget the most amazing benefits. These are the true advantages of democracy. ●●

Vol. 2 / Introduction
DEMOCRACY IN AMERICA
—Alexis de Tocqueville (1805-1859)

The three parties at the end of the street

66 Although war gratifies the army, it embarrasses and often exasperates the countless multitude of men whose minor passions every day require peace in order to be satisfied. Thus there is some risk of its causing, under another form, the disturbance it is intended to prevent.

Vol. 2 / Chapter XXII (Fourth Book)
DEMOCRACY IN AMERICA
—Alexis de Tocqueville (1805-1859)

●● I think it may be admitted as a general and constant rule, that, amongst civilized nations, the warlike passions will become more rare and less intense in proportion as social conditions shall be more equal. ●●

Vol. 2 / Chapter XXII (Fourth Book)
DEMOCRACY IN AMERICA
—Alexis de Tocqueville (1805-1859)

THE THIRD PARTY

❝ I had remarked during my stay in the United States, that a democratic state of society, similar to that of the Americans, might offer singular facilities for the establishment of despotism; and I perceived, upon my return to Europe, how much use had already been made by most of our rulers, of the notions, the sentiments, and the wants engendered by this same social condition for the purpose of extending the circle of their power. ❞

Vol. 2 / Chapter VI (FOURTH BOOK)
DEMOCRACY IN AMERICA
—Alexis de Tocqueville (1805-1859)

Those who, in the United States, are appointed to the direction of public affairs, are often inferior in capacity and in morality to those whom aristocracy would raise to power. But their interest is blended and identified with that of the majority of their fellow-citizens. They may therefore commit frequent breaches of trust, and serious errors; but they will never systematically adopt a tendency hostile to the majority; and it can never happen to them to give an exclusive or a dangerous character to their measures of government.

Vol. 1 / Introduction
DEMOCRACY IN AMERICA
—Alexis de Tocqueville (1805-1859)

PROSELYTISM

❝ I am, however, persuaded that anarchy is not the principal evil which democratic ages have to fear, but the least. For the principle of equality begets two tendencies; the one leads men straight to independence, and may suddenly drive them into anarchy; the other conducts them by a longer, more secret, but more certain road, to servitude. ❞

Vol. 2 / Chapter I (Fourth Book)
DEMOCRACY IN AMERICA
—Alexis de Tocqueville (1805-1859)

The late, late, show

THE HANDKERCHIEFS

●● I do not assert that men living in democratic communities are naturally stationary; I think, on the contrary, that a perpetual stir prevails in the bosom of those societies, and that rest is unknown there; but I think that men bestir themselves within certain limits beyond which they hardly ever go. They are for ever varying, altering, and restoring secondary matters; but they carefully abstain from touching what is fundamental. They love change, but they dread revolutions. ●●

Vol. 2 / Chapter XXI (THIRD BOOK)
DEMOCRACY IN AMERICA
—Alexis de Tocqueville (1805-1859)

WAR VIOLENCE VIOLENCE WAR

●● It is a mistake to believe that, when once the equality of conditions has become the old and uncontested state of society, and has imparted its characteristics to the manners of a nation, men will easily allow themselves to be thrust into perilous risks by an imprudent leader or a bold innovator. Not indeed that they will resist him openly, by well-contrived schemes, or even by a premeditated plan of resistance. They will not struggle energetically against him, sometimes they will even applaud him—but they do not follow him. To his vehemence they secretly oppose their inertia—to his revolutionary tendencies their conservative interests—their homely tastes to his adventurous passions—their good sense to the flights of his genius —to his poetry their prose. With immense exertion he raises them for an instant, but they speedily escape from him, and fall back, as it were, by their own weight. ●●

Vol. 2 / Chapter XXI (THIRD BOOK)
DEMOCRACY IN AMERICA
—Alexis de Tocqueville (1805-1859)

"AND NOW FOR MY NEXT TRICK, I WILL PASS THE HAT AMONG THE CROWD"

A brilliant achievement may win for you the favour of a people at one stroke; but to earn the love and respect of the population which surrounds you, requires a long succession of little services and obscure good offices, a constant habit of kindness, and an established reputation for disinterestedness. Local freedom, then, which leads a great number of citizens to value the affections of their neighbours, and of those with whom they are in contact, perpetually draws men back to one another, in spite of the propensities which sever them; and forces them to render each other mutual assistance.

Vol. 2 / Introduction, Page XXXIV
DEMOCRACY IN AMERICA
—Alexis de Tocqueville (1805-1859)

The
American dream

●● There is a love of country
which takes its rise principally
in the unreflecting, disinterested,
and undefinable sentiment
which attaches the heart of man
to the place of his birth. This
instinctive affection is blended
with the taste for old customs,
with the respect for ancestors,
and with historical recollections;
those who experience it cherish
their country with a feeling
resembling the love of our
paternal home. They love the
tranquillity which they enjoy
in it; they relish the peaceful

habits which they have contracted in it; they are attached to the recollections it affords them, and even find some pleasure in passing in it a life of obedience. This love of country often acquires a still more energetic character from religious zeal; and then it performs wonders. It is itself a kind of religion; it does not reason, it believes, feels, and acts. Nations have been known

to personify their country (if we may so speak) in the person of their prince. They have then transferred to him a part of the sentiments of which patriotism is composed; they have been proud of his power, and elated by his triumphs. 🌙🌙

Vol. 1 / Introduction, Pages XLV & XLVI
DEMOCRACY IN AMERICA
—Alexis de Tocqueville (1805-1859)

66 The especial taste which the men of democratic ages entertain for physical enjoyments is not naturally opposed to the principles of public order; nay, it often stands in need of order that it may be gratified. Nor is it adverse to regularity of morals, for good morals contribute to public tranquillity and are favourable to industry. It may even be frequently combined with a species of religious morality: men wish to be as well off as they can in this world, without forgoing their chance of another. 99

Vol. 2 / Chapter XI (SECOND BOOK)
DEMOCRACY IN AMERICA
—Alexis de Tocqueville (1805-1859)

DE ALBA-19

❝ There are two things which a democratic people will always find very difficult,—to begin a war, and to end it. ❞

Vol. 2 / Chapter XXII (THIRD BOOK)
DEMOCRACY IN AMERICA
—Alexis de Tocqueville (1805-1859)

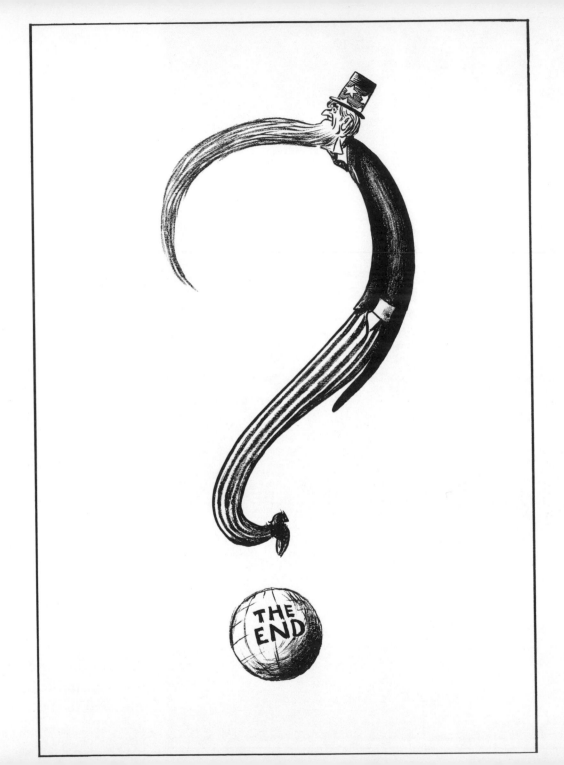

JOHN STUART MILL'S REVIEW (abridged)
of "Democracy in America" in the Westminster–London Review

In the opening of his work, Alexis de Tocqueville says, "Amongst the novel objects that attracted my attention during my stay in the United States, nothing struck me more forcibly than the general equality of conditions."

The capacity of co-operation for a common purpose, heretofore a monopolized instrument of power in the hands of the higher classes, is now a most formidable one in those of the lowest. Under these influences it is not surprising that society makes greater strides in ten years, towards the levelling of inequalities, than lately in a century, or formerly in three or four. Alexis de Tocqueville is unable to imagine that a progress, which has continued with uninterrupted steadiness for so many centuries, can be stayed now. He assumes that it will continue, until all artificial inequalities shall have disappeared from among mankind; those inequalities only remaining which are the natural and inevitable effects of the protection of property.

In "Democracy in America," de Tocqueville had chiefly in view the state of France, and much of it would be grossly exaggerated as a description of England: but we may receive it as a warning of what we may in time expect, if our influential classes continue to forego the exercise of the faculty which distinguishes rational creatures from brutes, and either blindly resist the course of events, or allow them to rush on wildly without any aid from human foresight:

"I perceive that we have destroyed those independent existences which were able to cope with tyranny single-handed: but the government has alone inherited the privileges of which families, corporations, and individuals have been deprived: to the strength, sometimes oppressive, but often conservative, of a few, has succeeded the weakness of all.

"If society is tranquil, it is not because it is conscious of its strength and of its well-being, but, on the contrary, because it believes itself weak and infirm, and fears that a single effort may cost it its life. Everybody feels the evil, but no one has courage or energy enough to seek the cure; the desires, the regrets, the sorrows, and the joys of the time produce no visible or premanent fruits."

In quoting so much of this passage, we would not be understood as adopting the whole and every part of it, as the expression of our own sentiments. The good which mankind have lost, is coloured, we think, rather too highly, and the evils of the present state of transition too darkly; and we think, also, that more than our author seems to believe, of what was good in the influences of aristocracy, is compatible, if we really wish to find it so, with a well-regulated democracy.

It is under the influence of such views that de Tocqueville has examined the state of society in America.

When de Tocqueville says that he studied America, not in order to disparage or to vindicate democracy, but in order to understand it, he makes no false claim to impartiality. Not a trace of a prejudice, or so much as a previous leaning either to the side of democracy or aristocracy, shows itself in his work. He is indeed anything but indifferent to the ends, to which all forms of government profess to be means. The good and evil of democracy, be they what they may, are what we must now look to; and for us the questions are, how to make the best of democracy, and what the best amounts to.

The conclusion at which he has arrived is, that this irresistible current, which cannot be stemmed, may be guided, and guided to a happy termination. The bad tendencies of democracy, in his opinion, admit of being mitigated; its good tendencies of being so strengthened as to be more than a compensation for the bad.

In a general way, the following may be given as a summary of de Tocqueville's opinion on the good and bad tendencies of democracy.

On the favourable side, he holds, that alone among all governments its systematic and perpetual end is the good of the immense majority. Were this its only merit, it is one, the absence of which could ill be compensated by all other merits put together. Secondly, no other government can reckon upon so willing an obedience, and so warm an attachment to it, on the part of the people at large. And, lastly, as it works not only *for* the people, but, much more extensively than any other government, *by means* of the people, it has a tendency which no other government has in the same degree, to call forth and sharpen the intelligence of the mass.

The disadvantages which our author ascribes to democracy are chiefly two:—First, that its policy is much more hasty and short-sighted than that of aristocracy. In compensation, however, he adds, that it is more ready to correct its errors, when experience has made them apparent. The second is, that the interest of the majority is not always identical with the interest of all; and hence the sovereignty of the majority creates a tendency on their part to abuse their power over all minorities.

The idea of a rational democracy is, not that the people themselves govern, but that they have *security* for good government. In a democracy only can there ever again be, on the part of the community generally, a willing and conscientious obedience to the laws.

BIOGRAPHICAL NOTES ON ALEXIS de TOCQUEVILLE*
by James Reeve (abridged) to his Translation of

"Democracy in America" by Alexis de Tocqueville

Tradition indeed relates that the village of Tocqueville owed its name to a Norman chief, or sea rover, called Toki, whose tumulus may still be seen on the high ground above the chateau.

The Chateau de Tocqueville consisted originally of what would be termed, north of the Tweed, a "peel" flanked by a huge tower of enormous solidity, and this part of the edifice is probably as old as the battle of Agincourt. Such was the type of the Norman manor-house of the fifteenth century.

At an early age the father of Alexis entered into possession of this inheritance, then surrounded with all its seignorial rights, and contracted a marriage with Mdlle. Lepeletier de Rosambo, a grand-daughter of M. de Malesherbes.

In 1805 Alexis, their third son, was born in Paris, but soon afterwards, being still an infant, he was brought to Tocqueville in a panier slung across a horse, with his nurse on a pillion. His education was scanty, having been conducted by an Abbe' Lesueur, whose death, during his absence in America, he affection-ately deplored. But that which was not scanty and not deficient was the high principle, the lofty conception of truth and duty, the unselfish dignity, with which his father, like himself, was completely imbued.

Alexis de Tocqueville was ten years old at the Restoration in 1815 and his father became successively prefect at Metz, at Amiens, and at Versailles. He was also raised, very deservedly, to the rank of a peer of France. These mutations had some effect on the earlier career of his son. In 1822 he gained the prize of rhetoric at the academy of Metz; and in 1827 he entered the profession of the magistracy, as Juge Auditeur at Versailles.

He was led, or rather compelled, to the study of democratic institutions not by any natural sympathy with popular agitation or any illusion as to the results of it, but by consternation at the ravages it had made during the Revolution of 1830; and by a deep-seated dread of its furthest consequences. Throughout his writings, throughout his parliamentary career, throughout his correspondence, the conviction may be traced that modern democracy tends to the establishment of absolute power, unless it be counteracted by a genuine love and practice of freedom. The modern theory of democracy is not so much a love of freedom as the love of a particular kind of power. Democratic power differs in its origin, but not at all in its nature, from other forms of absolutism.

Such were the views, still probably indistinct, which led the young "Juge Auditeur" to throw up his office at Versailles, and in the company of Gustave de Beaumont to proceed in 1831 to the United States. A mission was given them by Count Montalivet to examine the Penitentiary System, then recently introduced in America: they performed this part of their duty conscientiously; but the real motive of their journey was to examine the political institutions of the American people, and the result of it is the book entitled "Democracy in America."

De Tocqueville was not thirty years old when his great work appeared. He woke one morning, like Byron, and found himself famous. The success of the book was prodigious and it shortly afterwards opened

---

* *This biographical note is an abridgement of the Introductory Notice written by Henry Reeve for his translation of "Democracy in America."*

to Tocqueville the doors of the French Institute, and eventually of the Academy.

In 1837, when Alexis de Tocqueville had not been long settled in the old family chateau of his house, he came forward as a candidate for the representation of the *arrondissement* of Valognes in his own department. His reception was not very flattering. A trace of the old revolutionary prejudices lingered in the neighbourhood; a cry of *pas de nobles* was got up: his opponent, a retired cotton-spinner who had built a big house, said: "Prenez garde ! il va vous ramener les pigeons," pointing to the mighty dovecote of Tocqueville Manor; and, in short, the aristocratic though liberal candidate was defeated.

Two years later, at the general election of 1839, when de Tocqueville had made his way in the department, and had become an object of real attachment to his immediate neighbours and of respect to all the country round, he was elected to the Chamber of Deputies by a great majority, and he retained his seat under all circumstances as long as there was a free Parliament in France. A fixed idea of his was that the Constitution would be undermined by the democratic passions of the nation, and encroached upon by the insincerity of the Court, until nothing stable would remain, and the overthrow of the Parliamentary system would be followed at no distant time by the despotism of a single ruler.

At length the storm came. By no other man had it been so clearly foreseen, and for several months before the catastrophe he had carefully abstained from all participation in that mad system of agitation which produced the popular banquets and republican demonstrations of 1847. On the 27th January, 1848, soon after the opening of the last session of the Constitutional Parliament, he rose in the Chamber of Deputies, and said:—

"They tell me that there is no danger because there are no disturbances; they say that as there is no visible perturbation on the surface of society, there are no revolutions beneath it. Gentlemen, allow me to say that I think you wrong. Disturbance is not abroad, but it has laid hold of men's minds."

Within four weeks the explosion took place. The King fled. The Republic was proclaimed; and not only the Republic, but all the passions of a socialist revolution were let loose on France.

Then, indeed, neither Tocqueville nor any one of his political friends hesitated as to the part they were called upon to pursue. He had naturally been selected by the constituent body as one of the members of the Committee to frame the new Republican Constitution; and it is a curious example of the difficulty of governing human affairs that a Constitution, now universally acknowledged to be a masterpiece of absurdity, was the work of several men of undoubted intellectual power and political foresight. An attempt was made by Tocqueville to induce his colleagues to adopt the principle of a second Chamber; but this and every other attempt to construct the machinery of a true Republican Government utterly failed. The Republic was destined to a short-lived existence, between the frenzy of democratic socialism on the one hand, and the violence of that popular reaction which speedily assumed the name of Louis Napoleon Bonaparte.

In the summer of 1858 a more serious accident showed his lungs to be affected. In the autumn he was ordered to a milder climate than that of his own well-beloved domain. He repaired to Cannes, accompanied by the devoted partner of his life, and by one or two of his nearest relatives and friends.

On the 16th April, 1859, he expired. By his own express desire his mortal remains were interred in the churchyard of Tocqueville, and were attended to the grave by an immense assemblage, not of those who admired him for his genius, but of those who loved him for his goodness; and a plain cross of wood, after the fashion of the country, marks the spot where whatever of him was mortal lies.